AF717573

Poems from the Greek Anthology

Poems from the Greek Anthology

David R. Slavitt

The Sheep Meadow Press
Riverdale-on-Hudson, New York

Copyright © 2010 by David R. Slavitt

All rights reserved. No part of this publication may be reproduced or transmitted in any form or by any means, electronic or mechanical, including photocopy, recording, or any information storage and retrieval system, without permission in writing from the publisher, except in the case of brief quotations in reviews.

Designed and typeset by The Sheep Meadow Press.
Distributed by The University Press of New England.

All inquiries and permission requests should be addressed to the publisher:

The Sheep Meadow Press
PO Box 1345
Riverdale, NY 10471

Library of Congress Cataloging-in-Publication Data

Slavitt, David R., 1935-
Poems from the Greek anthology / David R. Slavitt.
p. cm.
ISBN 978-1-931357-73-9
I. Title.
PS3569.L3P64 2010
811'.54--dc22

2010035285

Some of the poems in this volume have appeared in *Boulevard* and *Per Contra,* to the editors of which the translator expresses his gratitude.

Contents

Translator's Preface

The Greek Anthology is a collection of some 4,000 poems assembled by Byzantine scholars nearly a thousand years ago. The poems range from the seventh century BC through to the renaissance of Greek culture in Byzantium in the sixth century AD. Some of the pieces are by the greatest names in Greek poetry, others are by obscure poets, and still others are anonymous. There are five volumes in Harvard University Press's Loeb Classical Library edition, with prose translations by W. R. Paton. Poets who have translated some of these wonderful pieces into English include Dudley Fitts (my teacher at Andover), Kenneth Rexroth, Robin Skelton, and Andrew Sinclair, while Peter Whigham's *Poems of Meleager,* and Tony Harrison's *Palladas: Poems* contain work of those poets that appear in the Anthology.

My practice here has been to riffle through the pages and find things that appeal to me, or that challenge me, or that I can figure out a way to bring into comfortable English. I have not been ambitious about anything like a systematic approach. It is my impression, however, that this random selection nevertheless represents fairly the frame of mind, the attitude, the tone of the whole collection. One goes into a bar, and the patrons are not the same on any given night, and the stories and jokes are different, but the bar has its own character and this, after a while, is why one goes there. These poems are epigrams, mostly in elegiac meter, and they are impish and indecorous, but there is an insight into the Greek spirit and experience that one doesn't get anywhere else. You need Homer and Aeschylus and Sophocles, but you need these, too, if only to learn how to laugh in Greek.

Poems from the Greek Anthology

An Epigram of Cyrillus

IX 369

For an epigram, two lines ought to do.
Even three? Well, perhaps. Four or more are a lapse.
What can one say of such epics *manquées?*

Menophilia's Mouth

Marcus Argentarius
V 105

Menophilia's mouth is simply heaven.
Look, there are Leda's Twins, Orion's sword—
and the Milky Way!

Catholicity

Nicarchus
V 38

What I like in a woman, Similus?
Amplitude, big tits and a fat ass.
Her age? That's not important.
If she's young she fucks. If she's old, she still sucks.

Achilles' Shield

Anonymous
IX 115

Intimate objects can object,
display animus, as did the shield
Odysseus won—and proud Ajax killed himself.

The Greek ships sailed;
Odysseus went down with his crew, near Corcyra;
and the shield Hephaistos made for Thetis' son

the sea floated off to wash ashore at Salamis,
at Ajax's tomb.

Reproach to a Stupid Courtier

Trajan
XI 418

Point your nose at the sun and open your mouth wide.
You'll be useful for telling time.

Etymology

IX 14

Phaedo noticed, sliding along in the shallows,
an octopus he poked and flipped with an oar
onto the beach grass where, in one of the hollows,
a rabbit had made its burrow close to the shore.

The octopus with a tentacle desperately seized
the rabbit and, in its mortal anguish squeezed
the creature to death, as Phaedo, astonished, watched
from nearby . . . and thus surf-and-turf was hatched.

Hummock

Isidorus of Aegae
VII 280

Not a hummock! This is a tomb. Farmer,
rein in your team; lift your plowshare,
for these are ashes. Here sow only tears.

Epitaph

Anonymous
VII 737

I lie here, a thrice unfortunate one:
slain,
          by a thief,
                              and mourned by none.

The Lamp

Statyllius Flaccus
V 5

I am the silver lamp that Flaccus gave
to Napé, to be her nightlight by her bed
where I gutter at her perfidies, her carnal displays
with many lovers.
                              And you, Flaccus,
you lie awake in the dark, imagining this.
Far apart, we burn together.

The Priest and the Lion

Antipater
VI 219

One of Cybele's priests took shelter from
a snowstorm in a cave that was dry, warm,
and safe, he thought, but the safety turned to fear,
as the lion that lived in the cave chanced to appear.
He sniffed at the priest with his huge nostrils and roared
and roared in thanks for a prey fortune had poured
down from heaven, apparently. The sound
filled the cave, echoing all around.
The priest cried out, a shriek of mortal fear,
but with the lion's roar, one could hardly hear
the human voice. Desperate he beat his drum,
sang and danced for his life. Surprised, overcome,
the lion, who'd never heard a drum before
was terrified. He did not wait for more
but turned and ran. The poor priest was relieved,
and forced to believe now what he'd said he believed.

Warning to Eros

Meleagar
V 57

You have burned my soul often enough! I say,
lay off! It has wings, too, and will fly away.

Sappho's Kisses

Paulus Silentiarus
V 246

Sappho's kisses are soft, and her arms and body
are soft, soft, but her heart—oh gods!—is hard.
She'll let you kiss her lips, but that's all. The rest
is forbidden fruit. It's Tantalus's torture.

Grapes

Anonymous
V 304

Your green grape, you refused me;
and your ripe grape, that too.
How about a nibble at your raisin?

The Garland

Rufinus
V 74

I send you these flowers, Rhodoclea,
that I wove with my own hands into a garland—
lilies, roses, anemones, fresh narcissus,
    and gleaming purple violets.
Wear it, but be not proud:
moment to moment, both of you are fading.

Epitaph for an Absurd Death

Anonymous
VII 543

Ah, Theogenes, the sea is treacherous,
and death is always sad, but to go that way,
on a heavily laden vessel that was swamped
when a sledge of tired cranes settled on it
out there in the Libyan sea, and sank it . . .
You all must have died laughing.

The Platonist

Callimachus
VII 471

Cleombrotus the Ambracian said, "Farewell,
Sun," and jumped from a high wall to enter Hades.
In despair? To escape an unbearable life?
                                                                No,
he'd read a treatise of Plato about the soul,
and believed it.

Coals

Asclepiades
V 210

Didyme waved at me and knocked me down,
and I melted like wax too close to a hot fire.
So what if she's black? So are the coals we light
that burn the same rosy-red inside.

The Contest

Rufinus
V 36

In one of those weird moods girls can get into,
Rhodope, Melita, and Rhodoclea
decided to compete about which of them had the prettiest cunt,
thank God choosing me to judge,
just as Paris had judged among the three goddesses.
They all stripped down, and . . . Good heavens!
Rhodope's Cyclops-eye gleamed like a flower
that glistened with morning dew.
Melita's was paler, almost mother-of-pearl,
and elegant, delicate lips that begged to be kissed.
Rhodoclea's was shiny, wet glass, almost dripping
and yet, at the same time, thirsty.
And which did I choose?
I knew that story of Paris and what a fix
his decision got him into. I told them, instead, the truth
that each of them was wonderful, wonderful, wonderful.

Old Flame

Rufinus
V 27

After all these years, suddenly you're nice,
bid me good-day, and smile, and those once smooth cheeks
are a web of cheerful wrinkles, while your ringlets
hang lank now, gone all salt-and-pepper.
You should have smiled at me years ago.
What I wanted, dear, was not brambles but rose buds.

Gold

Paulus Silentiarus
V 217

Zeus came to Danaë in a shower of gold,
and the meaning is clear that one draws from the old
tale. You're in love? You sigh? Never mind bouquets,
poems, or prayers in Aphrodite's powers.
Forget about all that romantic trash.
Bring cash.

The Oath

Antipater
VI 291

Bacchylis, as you know, is a party girl,
"Bacchus' sponge," they'd call her in admiration
for how much wine she could hold.
                                        When she fell sick,
she swore an oath to Demeter, if the goddess
could get her through the fever, to lay off the wine
"for the space of a hundred suns."
                                        It's a long time
to keep going on nothing but food and water.
But when she recovered, the witty girl took a sieve,
held it up, and, looking through its meshes,
saw at once those hundred suns. Done.

To Olympicus, the Boxer

Lucilius
XI 76

With a puss like that, Olympicus, keep away from mirrors,
and never look into clear water, like Narcissus.
You'll die, just like him, but from disgust.

Servant Girls

Rufinus
V 18

To hell with classy dames, so full of airs,
reeking of scent, and, if they show up, they bring
their maids, even into your bedroom.
Give me a slave girl every time. They smell of soap,
never talk about Homer, and are grateful
for a good time. What could be better than that?

Women, at their Best

Palladas
XI 381

Every woman has two shining moments:
in her bridal chamber when she gets laid,
and on her bier, when she gets laid out.

Diodorus

Nicarchus
XI 241

It's hard to tell whether Diodorus yawned or farted.
Above and below the stench is about the same.

A Bed of Pansies

Strato
XI 225

The bed has two insertors and two insertees,
but there are only three of them.
How so?
Like a see-saw, the one in the middle does double-duty.

Riddle

XIV 9

My father-in-law killed my husband;
my husband killed my father-in-law;
my brother-in-law killed my father-in-law;
and my father-in-law killed my father.
Who am I?

1. *Andromache.* Achilles, father of Pyrrhus, her second husband, killed Hector. Pyrrhus killed Priam. Paris killed Achilles. And Achilles killed Eetion, Andromache's father.

Skinny Marcus

Lucilius
XI 93

Using his head, skinny Marcus bored a hole
through one of Epicurus' atoms,
crawled inside it, and disappeared.

Checkers

XV 1

Palamedes, your bones should have been cut up
and made into checkers—not as a joke, but in honor
of the game you invented at Troy between the battles,
a better battle where friends could play at war.

On the Centaur, Chiron

Anonymous
XVI 115

A man without legs and feet, and a horse without a head.
Did horse belch up the man? Or did the man fart out the horse?

On Marcus' Book

XV 23

To fight off sadness,
depression, madness,
or a case of the blues,
unroll and peruse
this wonderful book,
in which you can look
at what will be,
what is, and has been.
And as you will see
in the lives of men
our joys and pains
our fears and desires
are burning fires
and nothing remains.

The Astrologer's Prediction

Agathias
XI 365

After Calligenes had put in his crop,
he came to consult Aristophanes, the astrologer,
to ask if he would get an abundant yield.
Aristophanes did some elaborate calculations
and then announced, "Yes, sir, absolutely,
providing that you get rain, and not too many weeds."
And then, as an afterthought, he added, "And no
frosts to hurt the plants. And no hail."
Calligenes was about to thank him, when he added,
"And you keep the goats out of the field."
With Calligenes halfway out the door,
he called out one further thought: "And you don't get locusts!"

Demophilus' Lullaby

Nicharcus
XI 186

The raven's song bodes death,
but when Demophilus sings,
the raven croaks.

Envy

Lucilius
XI 192

Envious Diophon, when he was crucified,
saw somebody near him on a higher cross,
which ruined his day.

Moron Joke

Lucian
XI 432

Why did the moron, when he was bitten by fleas, put out the lamp?
So they couldn't see him anymore.

The Nose

Theodorus
XI 198

To speak of Hermocrates' nose is absurd. You'd be calling
the large thing by the small. It's the nose's Hermocrates.

Note on an Apple

Plato
V 80

He who threw me to you loves you.
Consent, Xantippe,
before we both decay.

Conversation with Echo

Guaradas
XVI 152

Echo, I have a great favor to ask.
Ask.
I love her, but I do not think she loves.
She loves.
She never responds to my compliments and pleas.
Please!
You must help me. Tell her she owns my heart.
Art.
I'll give you a present for whatever you can do.
Can do!
I beg you. I'm desperate. Shall I abandon hope?
On, hope!

The Grammarian

Lucilius
XI 139

Zenonis keeps Menander, the grammarian, as tutor
to whom she has entrusted her little boy.
He never stops: all night it's conjugations,
active and passive, in every conceivable tense.

Love, the Candle-lighter

Rufinus
V 88

Light both candles, if you please.
If only one catches fire, either transfer the flame to the other
or else put out the first.

Warning to Sailors

Phalaecus
VII 650

Never go to sea.
If you want a long life, plow
behind a good team of oxen.
You don't find many sailors with gray hair.

A Drunkard's Complaint

Dionysius of Andros
VII 533

Of course I slipped and fell.
I was drunk. It was raining.
With both Bacchus and Zeus against me,
it was two gods against one mortal.

Epitaph for Dyonysius

Anonymous
VII 309

I, Dionysius of Tarsus, lie here,
sixty years old, and never married.
I wish my father hadn't either.

Springtime

Philodemus
IX 412

The roses are blooming, Sosylus,
the chickpeas are in, and the first cabbages,
smelts are running, and there's the new cheese . . .
But we don't go picnicking as we used to do
with our friends Antigenes and Bacchius.
We were all fooling around only yesterday,
and today we carry them to their graves.

Odysseus

Palladas
X 395

Odysseus said that nothing is better than homeland,
but that was before he tasted Circe's cheesecake,
good enough to make him forget ten Penelopes.

To a Rooster

Marcus Argenarius
IX 286

I was making love to Pyrrha, you stupid chicken,
and you woke me up with your crowing. That dream is gone!
Is this what I get for making you lord of the roost?
I'll wring your fucking neck and offer you up
on the altar of Serapis, god of dreams.

Death of an Eagle

Appolonides (or Philippus)
IX 264

A Cretan shot an eagle with an arrow,
but the eagle fell from the sky on that same Cretan
and pierced him with that arrow that killed him too.
No boasting, then, about Cretan marksmanship:
it's nothing compared to that of Zeus.

The Hardened Heart

Paulus Silentiarius
IX 443

Harden your heart so that all Love's arrows
bounce off. It's the only sure way.
If even the tip of his shaft finds some little chink . . .
Love knows that line, about putting it in just a little.

On a Whore's Bed of Laurel

Anonymous
IX 529

From the bed of one, in flight,
I'm anyone's for the night.

On an Unworthy Magistrate

Anonymous
IX 530

Why did Fortune give such advancement
to you, a fool, a crook, and arrogant, too?
To demonstrate her power!

World Traveler

Marcus Argentarius
V 63

Antigone, you were a homebody from Sicily,
but you have expanded our ambit widely.
Lately you keep asking for Samoa.
I'm thinking from Hungary. Yes, Pest.

To his Jug

Anonymous
V 135

Well-rounded, long-necked, and with a sweet mouth,
Bacchus' waitress, the Muses', and mine, too,
whenever I am sober, you are full,
and when I'm drunk, you're dry. What's up with that?
You seem to have no notion of conviviality.

Epitaph for a Bad-ass

Crinagoras
VII 401

This stone above a hateful head
crushes the bones of a son of a bitch.
Earth fills his lying mouth and little rat teeth,
weighs down his bowed legs, and crowns his bald pate.
The rest of him rots, but then he was rotten before.
The Earth has swallowed him up. We hope it won't vomit.

Secret Weapon

Ammonides
XI 201

In the battle against the Parthians,
if only we had shown them Antipatra, naked,
they'd have turned tail and run for their very lives.

The Painter

Lucilius
XI 215

Eutychus, the painter, was father of twenty sons,
not one of them his likeness.

The Pedophile

Lucilius
XI 217

Hoping to fool us, Appolophanes got married
and announced in the marketplace that tomorrow
he would have a child.
Just as we feared.

Valediction

Ammianus
XI 226

May the dust lie lightly upon you, Nearchus,
so dogs can dig you up and gnaw your bones.

In Defense of Nicylla

Lucilius
XI 68

Some say you dye your hair, Nycilla, but not so!
It's just as black as the day you bought it!

Melissa

Marcus Argentarius
V 32

Ah, Melissa, you are one honey-bee,
dripping sweetest nectar from every kiss,
and then, of course, there's the sting of settling up.

Nicon's Nose

Nicarchus
XI 406

That's Nicon's nose,
and I suppose
that Nicon, too,
will heave into view
in a little while.
It's less than a mile
that it comes before
the rest of the guy.
And he will get here,
by and by.

Charlotte

Ammianus
XI 231

The initial, penultimate, and last letters? Misleading!
But after a night's work, there's the last five's tang.

Lollianus

Lucian
IX 274

So he's dead, is he? Among the silent shades . . .
But Lollianus, silent? Isn't he still explaining
one damn thing or another to all the ghosts?
What I most fear about death now is meeting him
and having to listen again to his endless blather

Gay Pride

Strato
XII 245

Any dumb animal can fuck.
But we humans, ingenious and intelligent,
invented buggery.
Those poor bastards captivated by women
are no better than beasts.

Timon, the Misanthrope

Callimachus
VII 317

Timon, now that you're dead, which do you hate more,
the darkness or the light?
Darkness. Even more are in Hades.

The Miser

Nicarchus
XI 169

Dinarchus, the miser, decided to hang himself yesterday.
All he needed was a quarter's worth of rope.
He tried to bargain with the shopkeeper, but no go.
So he still lives

Table d'Hôte

Leonidas of Alexandria
XI 9

I'm full to groaning, and the food just keeps on coming—
like rain after the harvest is in
or fair winds after the ship is safe in port.

Metaphysical Speculation

Anonymous
X 118

How was I born, where did I come from?
Why am I here? Where will I go?
I came from nothing and shall be nothing again.
I know nothing and have learned nothing.
Men are worthless. I am worthless.
Pass the wine. That'll cure it all.

Diogenes

Antiphilus of Byzantium
XVI 333

Pouch, cloak, barley cake, stick,
and a cup were what the Cynic thought would suffice
for life's needs. But then he saw a farmer
drink from his palm.
Admiring such refinement,
he asked of the cup, "What do I need you for?"

Gessius

Palladas
XVI 317

Look at that marvelous stone bust of Gessius,
absolutely dumb—just like him.

Pan's Warning

Nicarchus
IX 330

I am the goat-footed Pan
Simo erected to guard this spring.
Drink as much as you like, even fill your pitcher.
But that's it. No washing your filthy feet.
You see my enormous prick? I'll shove it up your ass.
Unless you're the kind that likes that kind of thing,
in which case, I'll take my club, which is even larger,
and break your fucking head.

Down

Alcaeus
XII 30

The down on your legs, Nicander, is coming out
kinky, and creeping upward, too When your ass
is hairy, too, your lovers will be fewer.
Youth is fleeting. It's very sad, but sure.

Flora Dora

Dionysius, the Sophist
V 81

Those roses you're holding out, are they offered for sale?
Or are you, my dear? Or, on a good day, both?

The Astrologer

Lucilius
XI 163

Aulus, the astrologer, made his own chart
and announced that his hour had come: he would pass away
in exactly four hours. The four hours passed,
and then five,
and refusing to live in ignorance and shame
he hanged himself.

Astrologers, the Lot of Them

Lucilius
XI 160

All the astrologers said that my father
would live to a fine old age.
Or all but one.
Hermoclides said that my father would die young,
but he said this at his wake.

Toast

Rufinus
V 12

Let's drink to each other, Prodike, while we still can.
Age waits in the shadows, and behind it, death.

House Rules

Lucilius
XI 10

These are the rules of my little soirées, Aulus,
and you're invited, but only if you obey them.
No fucking poetry. That's the first.
And rule two: no talk about poetry, either.

The Larder

Callicter
XI 5

Cakes, pies, loaves of wheaten bread
that you can't remember paying for?
                                        Wise up,
and ask if your wife might be giving the baker a roll?

Apis, the Prizefighter

Lucilius
XI 80

His opponents set up this statue to Apis, the boxer,
with thanks.
He never laid a knuckle on any of them.

The Long and the Short of It

Attributed to Julian the Apostate
XI 108

Conon is four feet tall, and his wife nearly six.
Head to head his toes are in it.
Foot to foot, his nose is in it.

Dr. Smartheim

Palladas
XI 305

Fool! Jackanapes. Sapinpaw to a pissant!
The grammarians think you're a wise philosopher.
The philosophers say you're an able grammarian.
What this suggests is that you are a total impostor,
a multi-talented, monstrous pig's pizzaza.

Investor

Antiphanes
XI 168

You poor bastard, you look at the calendar with such lust,
calculating your wealth at compound interest,
which is Time's gift. But Time is not your friend,
and never having drunk wine or wreathed your temples
in pretty garlands, or dallied at love, you will die
with only the coins they put on a dead man's eyes.

"Savior"

Nicarchus
XI 331

Philo called his leaky tub "Savior,"
but not even Zeus himself could be saved in it.
His passengers sailed in a very the narrow passage,
the shore on one hand and on the other Hades.

Sweet and Bitter

Cillactor
V 29

Nothing in all the world is sweeter than pussy,
until it wants money, and then it's black hellebore.

Vintage

Philodemus
V 13

Sixty, if she's a day,
her hair is as thick and as dark as it ever was,
and her marvelous breasts are still firm.
Her skin isn't wrinkled but smooth and sweet smelling.
Don't dismiss, Charito, my lads, she's still
one heavenly fuck.

Warning

Rufinus
V 41

He beat you and turned you out of the house half-naked?
Poor dear, was he blind, and with a heart of stone?
Did he find you with a lover? Well, that happens
to all women, at one time or another.
Don't fret about it too much, but next time, sweetheart,
maybe you'll remember to bolt the door?

Another Riddle

XIV 40

There are two sisters, but each gives birth to the other,
so they are mother and daughter as well as sisters.[1]

Strategic Problems

Agathias Scholasticus
V 302

It's tough to get laid. If you look in the streets for a hooker
you'll find that they charge a hell of a lot. And virgins
want to be wooed and married, which is even more
expensive. You could wake up your own wife,
but she's even more reluctant than you are.
Adultery, then? That's sinful and dangerous.
Widows
are either too easy, which isn't much fun
(and she knows every hooker's trick), or else too tough
and so ashamed she's boring. Your household servants?
Then you've changed places and you are the servant.
Somebody else's servant then? No good:
it's against the law and shameful. What can you do?
Learn from wise Diogenes. Go without.

---

1. Day and night.

Grammarian's Complaint

Palladas of Alexandria
IX 165

I start each day in the schoolroom with Achilles' wrath,
and come home at night to my wife and yet more wrath.

The Vine and the Goat

Leonidas of Tarentum
IX 99

The billy goat got into the vineyard
and ate all the leaves off a vine, which then addressed him:
"My stem is yet untouched, and I will produce
more leaves and grapes, which men shall turn into wine
to pour in libation when they cut your wicked throat."

On the Double Bath

Paulus Silentiarus
IX 620

The men bathe here on one side of the gate,
and, on the other, the women.
Love can't make it through, but idea does—
which is almost as good and sometimes even better.

Dr. Kronkheit

Nicarchus
XI 113

Marcus, the physician, touched the statue of Zeus.
A marble statue, right? And of Zeus, the god?
Even so, they're burying it today.

The Orthopod

Callicter
XI 120

Socles promised to straighten Diodorus' crooked back.
He put three heavy stones, each four feet square,
on the patient's spine. They crushed him, and he died.
But his corpse's back is as straight now as a schoolboy's ruler.

Death of a Poet

Lucilius
XI 133

Eutychides is dead.
You shades who dwell under the earth, I send you
warning. He is on his way. With odes.
He ordered that twelve lyres be burnt with him,
and twenty-five cases of music. Flee, if you can!
And for us, who are still on the good side of the grass,
the idea of death is now even more fearsome.

Title Deed

Anonymous
IX 74

I was once Achaemenides' field.
I'm Menippus' now, and one day I'll be someone else's.
Achaemenides thought he owned me. So did Menippus.
But I belong to no man. Only to Fortune.

Farewell

Leonidas of Tarentum
VII 452

Eubulus, the teetotaler, is gone.
Let us drink to his memory. And again and again,
before we join him.

A Soldier's Death

Apollonides
VII 233

Aelius, the captain, with many medals in his cabinet,
had fallen ill and knew his end was at hand,
so he took his sword and drove it into his belly
to keep Disease from boasting of a triumph.

Confession

Palladas
XI 341

People adore praise; the unvarnished truth
won't win you any friends. Still, to deliver
a well-deserved insult . . . It's Attic honey!

An Epitaph for Macho

Discorides
VII 708

O Earth, lie light on Macho's grave
and let your ivy wreathe his marker.
A wit, a gadfly whose stings were all the darker
for the laughter they provoked, he was a brave
and worthy practitioner. Athenians may smile,
but he brought poetry's tang here to the Nile.

Happy Face

Anonymous
VII 621

My name, too, was Sophocles. I entered
the house of Hades grinning or, say, with a rictus.
Sardinian celery[1], the poison herb I ate,
produces muscular spasms and will do that.
But don't you grin. You may not go that way
but, one way or another, you surely will go.

Portrait of Theodote

Julianus, Prefect of Egypt
VII 565

He got her to the life.
Had he been less good, those of us who mourn her
could forget her a little and feel less pain.

---

1. A source of strychnine.

Conversation with a Ghost

Callimachus
VII 524

"Is that you, Charidas?"
                    "Yes, the son of Arimmas of Cyrene."
"So what's it like down there?"
                    "Very dark."
"And the stories about coming back . . . ?"
                    "All lies."
"And Pluto?"
                    "A myth!"
"There's no good news? Nothing to hope for?"
                    "Well, down here, meat is cheap."

Epitaph for Fallen Heroes

Simonides
VII 442

Let us remember the men who are here entombed:
not one of them turned away; they fell in battle
defending their home, Tegea, rich in flocks.
Their armor may be gone, but no one can ever
strip from their white skulls the crowns of freedom.

Epitaph for Gorgias

Anonymous
VII 134

Here lies Gorgias, the Cynic.
Resting in peace?
At least he's stopped clearing his throat and blowing his nose.

The Philosopher's Diet

Palladas of Alexandria
IX 170

My belly is shameless, but I can reason with it
and persuade it to temperance by logical argument.
The intellect is a higher power than the gut,
so there should be no problem. Right? Right?

On Hearing the Bad News

Callimachus
VII 80

I just heard that you died—and some time ago.
I was moved to tears.
I remember our many long talks, Heraclitus,
bright and lively, even as the light failed.
And now you lie moldering in the ground,
and have turned to dust.
Still, Hades, who seizes everything,
won't lay a hand on your "Nightingales,"
which will keep on singing—as will you.

Fortune's Temple

Palladas
IX 182

Mistress of ups and downs, now it's your turn:
your temple is turned to a tavern, and you, too,
must enroll in the course you teach
in the school of hard knocks.

The Roman Months

Anonymous
IX 580

I install the consuls to
their offices.
I plough the fields.
The month for starting war is who
I am.
In April the weather yields
to springtime. I'm May—I bring roses.
I am the month of June and I
deliver lilies. July discloses
bound sheaves of wheat for our food supply.
By August are the south winds vexed
so that the Nile overflows its banks.
Then with September come the grapes
October turns to wine in tanks.
In November all that oil escapes
from the olive press. To end the year
December brings for our delectation
the flutes and lyres that give cheer
to Saturnalia's celebration.

The Climb

Honestus
IX 230

It's steeper than it looks, and you ascend
Helicon laboriously. But after a while,
longer than you expected, you get there
and drink the sweet water of Pegasus' spring.
Then you see how it all makes sense: study
is all up-hill, but the gift of the Muses is sweet.

The Honey Trap

Meleager
V 24

It's a terrible idea, as I ought to have learned
from the tears, the rages, the jealousies we've been through.
I should know better, and Heliodora herself
warns me to leave her alone, but still, but still,
she punctuates her words of warning with kisses.

Epitaph for a Weaver

Leonidas of Tarentum
VII 726

Old Plathis, early up and late to bed,
worked at her weaving to earn her crusts of bread,
singing a tune as she wove, sometimes until dawn,
doing Athena's careful work upon
her battered loom. She smoothed with a wrinkled hand
on a wrinkled knee yet another bright strand
for the hungry shuttle—until she was eighty years old.
Now that hand of hers is stilled and cold.

Preferences

Strato
XII 5

What do I prefer in a young boy?
Pale is good, but darker is also fine.
Blond is terrific, but also brown and black.
And the eyes? They should be blue. Or a nice deep brown.

Justification

Strato
XII 15

When Graphicus was sitting in his tub
a plank pinched his delicious tush.
How am I to resist, if even wood feels desire?

The Physician's Reputation

Callicter
XI 118

Dr. Phidon did not treat me
or even examine me, for that matter.
But, feeling poorly, I remembered his name
and died.

The Decedent's Wishes

Anonymous
XI 8

No wreathed flowers, no incense and no fires.
Don't waste your money: they don't do any good.
When I'm alive, give me all the presents you like,
but afterwards? Don't pour good wine on the earth.
It turns into mud. Not even the dead drink that.

Epitaph for Sardanapallus

Anonymous
VII 325

Whatever I ate or drank, and whatever I learned,
and all those I loved, I still have.
My rich possessions? They're gone, but then who needs them?

Epitaph of Epictetus, the Philosopher

Anonymous
VII 676

I was a slave and shaky in my limbs.
I was as poor as Irus[1] in the *Odyssey.*
I had so little. But the gods loved me.

The Winner

Anyte
VII 490

Hearing of her stunning beauty and great virtue,
many suitors came to Antibia's house
but, shouldering his way through them all, Fate took her.

1. The begger in Book XVIII.

An Epitaph for Myself

Meleager
VII 417

I was born in Gadara to Syrian Greeks.
My father was Eucrates. I grew up in Tyre,
where I started writing Menippian combinations
of verse and prose.
                                        But am I a Syrian, really?
One chaos gave birth to the whole universe: we all
live in the world together.
                                                  Now, in old age,
I write these lines with the last of my strength, for age
and death are near neighbors. Only wish me well,
the gabby geezer I am. And, in return,
I wish that you, too, may live to be one someday.

Beaver

Julian Antecessor
XI 368

That's some beard, bud.
Way beyond razors.
Even beyond scissors.
What you need is a goddamn scythe.

The Miser's Dream

Macedonius the Consul
XI 366

The miser dreamt that he had found a treasure,
so he wanted to die while he was still asleep.
But dawn broke, the beautiful dream faded,
and in pitiless daylight he was poor again.
What could he do then but go back to bed?

Gray Hair

Anonymous
XI 420

Those gray hairs of yours bespeak wisdom,
unless, of course, you speak. Then they're just hairs.

The Grammarian and the Doctor

Lucian
XI 401

A doctor sent his son to me for lessons,
and we began with the wrath of Achilles
and how it hurled many valiant souls to Hades.
The doctor stopped the lessons. He said that the boy
could learn as well at home from him: he knew
much more than I about sending souls to Hades.

A Prayer

Anonymous
X 108

O Zeus, give us good things,
whether we pray for them or not.
And keep evil things from us,
even if we pray for them.

Standards

Meleager
XII 41

Thero is no good any more,
and Apollodotus is ruined.
They gleamed like fire once but are burnt-out torches,
all hairy now and fit only for goat-fuckers.

The Slowest Runner

Nicarchus
XI 82

In the long race in Arcadia, poor Charmus
against five others managed to come in seventh.
"Seventh?" you ask. "How in the world was that?"
He had a friend who joined him in street clothes
to urge him on: "Faster, Charmus, faster!"
So Charmus finished seventh. With five more friends,
he'd have come twelfth.

Sextus' Picture

Anonymous
XI 145

If Sextus' picture declaims,
Sextus never has anything to say.
The picture then is the rhetor,
and the rhetor is the picture of the picture.

Crito

Lucilius
XI1 65

When Crito the skinflint has a sour stomach,
he doesn't take penny mints: he sniffs a penny.

Death of a Sailor

Antipater of Sidon
VII 625

Diodorus, son of Calligenes,
of Olynthus, the master mariner,
knew the Gates of Heracles
and the waters around Crete.
He'd piloted the Thracian Sea.
                                        And now?
He's drowned in port, drunk, falling off the prow
of his moored ship. After all that deep blue water,
this little bit in the harbor did him in.

Pyrrho, the Sceptic

Julianus, Prefect of Egypt
VII 576

A) Are you dead, Pyrrho?
                                        B) Maybe.
A) Even after they've buried you, can you doubt?
                                        B) Maybe.
A) Oh, come off it! The tomb puts an end to doubt.

Director's Note

Palladas
X 72

The world's a stage, &c. Just read your lines
and do what the script requires of you. Don't sweat it.
If you take it too much to heart, the pains will feel real.

Praise of the Twin Goddesses

Macedonius the Consul
X 67

Hail Memory! Hail Forgetfulness!
The one for keeping hold of whatever is good,
and the other for letting go of whatever is isn't.

Skinflint

Lucian
XI 397

Artemidorus is rich. With his fat billfold
he never spends a dime. Living this way
he's like a mule burdened with much gold
that subsists on hay.

An Old Story

Automedon
XI 29

Your love-bunny is on her way! What now?
It's a hell of a fix you're in, Automedon. Your rod
is limp as a boiled carrot.
She'll laugh at you as you try to put to sea,
an oarsman without an oar.

Favorinus

Meleager
XI 223

Does old Favorinus still have sex? Oh, yes,
he assured me that he does with his own mouth.

About the Author

DAVID R. SLAVITT is the translator of *The Theban Plays of Sophocles* (Yale University Press), Ovid's *Metamorphoses* (Johns Hopkins University Press), *The Book of the Twelve Prophets* (Oxford University Press), and Ariosto's *Orlando Furioso* (Harvard University Press). He is coeditor of the Johns Hopkins *Complete Roman Drama in Translation* series and the *Penn Greek Drama* series. His most recent collections of his own poetry include *The Seven Deadly Sins and Other Poems* and *Change of Address: Poems, New and Selected.* His translation of *Selected Poems* by Manuel Bandeira was published by Sheep Meadow Press. He has taught at Princeton and the University of Pennsylvania.